I'M NOT BEING FUNNY

by Piers Black

I'm Not Being Funny was first performed at
the Bush Theatre, London, on 7 May 2026.

I'M NOT BEING FUNNY

by Piers Black

Cast

Billie	Tia Bannon
Peter	Jerome Yates

Creative Team

Writer	Piers Black
Director	Bryony Shanahan
Producer	Rebecca Prentice
Set & Costume Designer	Amelia Jane Hankin
Lighting Designer	Lucía Sánchez Roldán
Sound Designer & Composer	Asaf Zohar
Intimacy Director	Tommy Ross Williams
Casting Consultant	Fran Cattaneo
Associate Producer	Alice Linnane
Production Manager	Harry Fearnley-Brown for New Wolf Productions
Stage Manager	Roni Neale
Stage Management Placement	Liza Evers

For Bush Theatre

Lead Producer	Emma Halstead
Lead Dramaturge	Olivia Poglio-Nwabali
Marketing Campaign Lead	Karishma Kaur
Technical Manager	Jamie Haigh

I'm Not Being Funny is produced by Prentice Productions, in association with Bush Theatre.

CAST

Tia Bannon | Billie

Tia trained at RADA.

Theatre includes: *Seven Methods of Killing Kylie Jenner* (Woolly Mammoth/Public Theatre/Royal Court); *Oresteia/ Hamlet* (Park Avenue Armory & Almeida); *Faith, Hope and Charity workshop* (National Theatre); *Losing Venice* (Orange Tree); *Dead Don't Floss* (National Theatre); *Abigail* (The Bunker); *The Winter's Tale*; *Pericles* (both Shakespeare's Globe); *Camelot: The Shining City* (Sheffield Theatres).

Television includes: *Babies*; *Prime Target*; *Father Brown*; *Acrimonious*; *Shakespeare and Hathaway*; *Midsomer Murders*; *This Is A Relationship*; *Shakespeare Uncovered*.

Film includes: *The Surrogate*; *Stitch Head*; *Milk*; *Maintenance Required*; *Thanks For Considering Me*; *Seven Methods of Killing Kylie Jenner*; *Good Morning, Midnight*; *The Drifters*; *Dead End*; *Lynch*; *Balls*; *Nightless*; *Oxygen & Terror*.

Radio and Voice Work includes: *The Bacchae*; *Intimacy*; *Pygmalion*; *Bleak House*; *Harry Potter*; *Camberwell Green*; *Martians*; *Relativity 2, 3 & 4*.

Jerome Yates | Peter

Theatre includes: *Driftwood* (Pentabus/ThickSkin); *Pinocchio* (Watermill); *Our Teacher's A Troll, Peter Pen and the Battle for Neverland* (Ruined Theatre); *Surfacing* (Asylum Arts); *The Leftovers, Sophocles' Oedipus/ Silent Practice, We Anchor in Hope, Against, Julius Caesar, Jumpers for Goalposts, Much Ado About Nothing, Three Sisters, The Glass Menagerie* (LAMDA).

Television includes: *Project Codename*.

Film includes: *The Children*.

CREATIVE TEAM

Piers Black | Writer

Piers is a writer and director, and Artistic Director of award-winning Ransack Theatre. His play *My Dad Hunts Bears* was a finalist for the Papatango Prize and developed on attachment at the National Theatre Studio. His show *Catching Comets* was nominated for a Fringe First, won an OffComm Award, and toured nationally following its Edinburgh Fringe premiere. He won the BBC Alfred Bradley Bursary Award with his radio play *Human Resources*, later broadcast on BBC Radio 4 as Drama of the Week.

Piers' most recent play *I'm Not Being Funny* was performed at Bush Theatre from 7 May–13 June 2026, before transferring to Bristol Old Vic's Weston Studio from 23–27 June 2026.

Other work has been staged at HighTide, Royal Exchange, HOME and the Bolton Octogon. He has been invited to the Soho Theatre Writers' Lab and BBC Northern Voices, shortlisted for the Kudos Writers' Award, the Alpine Fellowship, and named a finalist in the Shore Script Short Film competition.

As a director, Piers has worked at the National Theatre, Almeida, Royal Exchange, Lyric Hammersmith, HOME, The Yard, Theatre503 and Soho. He is currently developing new work with the National Theatre Studio and The Lowry.

Bryony Shanahan | Director

Bryony is a freelance theatre director. Between 2019 and 2023, she was Joint Artistic Director of the Royal Exchange Theatre, Manchester and was recently Associate Director at The Traverse.

Theatre includes: As Director for the Royal Exchange: *Bloody Elle* (also Traverse/Soho/ West End), *No Pay? No Way!*, *Beginning, Let The Right One In, Nora: A Doll's House, Wuthering Heights, Queens of the Coal Age, Weald, Nothing.*

As Director: *Standing in the Shadows of Giants, Same Team, Enough* (Traverse); *Keli* (National Theatre of Scotland); *Beauty and the Beast* (Northern Stage); *Trade* (Young Vic); *Chicken Soup* (Sheffield); *Operation Crucible* (59E59 NYC/ Sheffield Crucible/ UK tour); *Bitch Boxer* (UK tour).

Rebecca Prentice | Producer

Founded in 2023 by producer Rebecca Prentice, Prentice Productions develops bold new writing across theatre, film, and audio. Often focusing on female-led storytelling, the company is driven to innovate within the arts at a time of limited resources, creating work that is both socially relevant and commercially ambitious.

Theatre includes: *How I Learned to Swim* (Paines Plough's Roundabout/Bristol Old Vic/Brixton House); *Jobsworth* (Pleasance Edinburgh, Park transfer 2025, with TV development at Brock Media); *30 and Out* (Soho/ Pleasance London/Pleasance Edinburgh/Omnibus); *Mermaid* (Theatre503).

Screen includes: the award-winning *House Hunters* (screened at BFI Flare and multiple BIFA and BAFTA-qualifying festivals); *The Pirate* (winner of four awards including Best Story); *Driving with Tim* (starring Simon Callow); *Game Over* (in post-production), alongside two features in pre-production and three scripts in development.

Rebecca is supported by the MGCFutures Bursary and the Stage One Bursary for New Producers.

Amelia Jane Hankin | Set & Costume Designer

Amelia trained in Architecture and at the Royal Academy of Dramatic Art then RSC. Amelia has designed a variety of theatre ranging from new writing, devised, touring theatre, immersive, site-specific, community and theatre for young people. Amelia is an Associate Lecturer at the RCA and co-founded the Office for Speculative Spatial Design in 2020.

Design includes: *Standing in the Shadow of Giants* (Traverse); *The Crucible, Othello* (The Globe); *Wolves on Road* (Bush); *Red Pitch* (Soho Place & Bush); *Limp Wrist and the Iron Fist, Cinderella* (Brixton House); *Mlima's Tale* (Kiln); *Richard III* (Liverpool Playhouse); *Holes* (Theatre Royal Bury St Edmunds); *Let The Right One In, Mountains* (Royal Exchange); *Drowntown* (Barbican), *The Night Before Christmas* (Leeds Playhouse); *The Wave, (This Isn't) A True Story* (Almeida); *Christmas in the Sunshine, The Wolf The Duck and The Mouse* (Unicorn); *Unknown Rivers* (Hampstead); *Sing Yer Heart Out For The Lads* (Chichester Festival); *One Under* (Graeae), *Blue Orange* (Birmingham Rep); *The Comedy of Errors* (RSC); *The Fishermen* (Trafalgar Studios); *Gastronomic* (Curious Directive); *PowerPlay* (Historic Royal Palaces); *Good Dog* (UK tour); *Rudolf* (West Yorkshire Playhouse), *Fake It 'Til You Make It* (UK & Australian tour); *We Are You* (Young Vic).

Studio AJH is based in Hackney, London.

Lucía Sánchez Roldán | Lighting Designer

Lucía is a lighting designer working in theatre. She trained in Technical Theatre and Stage Management at RADA after completing a degree in Natural Sciences. She is the joint winner of the 2019 ALD Michael Northen Award for Lighting Design and received the MGCfutures bursary in 2021.

Theatre includes: *The Waves, The EU Killed My Dad* (Jermyn Street); *Vincent in Brixton* (Orange Tree); *The Manningtree Witches, The Importance of Being Earnest* (Mercury, Colchester); *Petty Men, Dear Martin, Black el Payaso* (Arcola); *Angels on the Underground, Girl in the Machine* (Young Vic); *Radiant Boy, How to Succeed in Business Without Really Trying, The Walworth Farce* (Southwark Playhouse); *Bad Lads* (Live Theatre/tour); *Sisters 360* (Polka); *Mog's Christmas* (Royal & Derngate); *Bedroom Farce* (Queens); *Kill Thy Neighbour* (Theatre Clwyd & Torch); *Papercut* (Park); *Under Milk Wood* (Sherman); *The Wonderful World of Dissocia* (Theatre Royal Stratford East); *Forest Awakens/Code and Dagger, A New Beginning* (Kiln); *Orpheus Descending* (National Theatre of Tirana).

As Associate Lighting Designer: *Evita, Hello, Dolly!* (London Palladium); *The Lehman Trilogy, Stranger Things: The First Shadow, Amélie* (West End); *Drive Your Plow Over the Bones of the Dead* (International tour); *Cabaret* (Playhouse); *two palestinians go dogging* (Royal Court).

Asaf Zohar | Sound Designer & Composer

Asaf studied composition at the Royal College of Music.

Theatre includes: *Ballet Shoes* (National Theatre, nominated for Olivier Award - Outstanding Musical Contribution); *Victoria* (Watermill); *The Estate* (National Theatre); *Measure for Measure* (RSC); *The Shitheads* (Royal Court); *Macbeth* (Wessex Grove, UK & US tour); *My Mother's Funeral: The Show* (Paines Plough, UK & US tour); *God of Carnage* (Lyric Hammersmith); *The Meat Kings! (Inc.) of Brooklyn Heights* (Papatango Prize Winner), *Disruption*, *The Shape of Things*, *Farewell Mister Haffman* (Park); *The Bleeding Tree*, *Captain Amazing*, *Here* (Papatango Prize Winner), *The Bit-Players*, *Romeo and Juliet* (Southwark Playhouse); *Nanny* (Bristol Old Vic); *Some Demon* (Arcola, Papatango Prize Winner); *Waiting for Anya* (The Barn); *Bright Half Life* (King's Head); *Dennis of Penge* (Guildhall School of Music and Drama); *SORRY, YOU'RE NOT A WINNER* (Paines Plough/Bristol Old Vic/ Theatre Royal Plymouth); *Wild Country* (Camden People's); *SESSIONS* (Paines Plough/ Soho Theatre); *The Silence and the Noise* (Papatango Theatre Company); *Peter Pan Reimagined* (Birmingham Rep); *Whitewash* (Soho); *Dennis of Penge* (Albany Deptford/ Ovalhouse); *Peter Pan and the Battle for Neverland* (Ruined Theatre); *The Goose Who Flew* (Half Moon); *The Shadowpunk Revolutions* (Edinburgh Fringe).

Television includes: *Reggie Yates: Extreme Russia, Race Riots USA, Reggie Yates: Extreme UK, Dispatches: Taliban Child Fighters, Reggie Yates: Extreme South Africa*, in addition to in-house work for Virgin Media and various media companies. Previous film work was shown at Cannes, BAFTA, Edinburgh and Encounters festivals.

Tommy Ross Williams | Intimacy Director

Tommy (they/them) came to intimacy direction through their extensive experience in developing safer spaces in the arts and their commitment to embodied practice. They are a BECTU IC Registry Level 2 Intimacy Coordinator and former chair of the IC BECTU branch.

Theatre includes: *Broken Glass* (Young Vic); *Brokeback Mountain*, *Little Big Things* (@SohoPlace); *Two Gentlemen of Verona* (RSC); *Positive* (Southwark Playhouse); *Tender* (Bush); *Glass Menagerie* (Rose Theatre Kingston/UK tour); *Just For One Day* (The Old Vic); *As You Like It* (Shakespeare's Globe); *Salty Irina* (Roundabout @Summerhall).

Television includes: *Love Is Blind UK*; *Married at First Sight UK*; *Honey*; *Knight of the Seven Kingdoms*; *I, Jack Wright*; *Sweetpea*; *Juice*; *Slow Horses*; *Citadel*; *Outrageous*; *Human*.

Film includes: *The Fantastic Four: First Steps*; *Black Church Bay*; *Ish*; *Love and Rage: Munroe Bergdorf*.

Fran Cattaneo | Casting Consultant

Fran is a London-based casting director, who has assisted in the offices of Rory Okey, Dan Hubbard and Heather Basten for screen and Harry Blumenau, Lotte Hines at the Donmar Warehouse and Stuart Burt for stage. She recently worked as an Associate with Charlotte Sutton on the New York premiere of *Wild Rose*.

Theatre includes: As Casting Director: *Maggots* (Bush); *Fxfest Readings* (Soho); Selina Thompson's Twine (Yard); *The Bleeding Tree* directed by Stage Debut-winning Director Sophie Drake (Southwark Playhouse); *The Great Privation: How To Flip Ten Cents Into A Dollar* (Theatre503).

As Casting Consultant: *I'm Not Being Funny*, *…blackbird hour*, *This Might Not Be It* (Bush).

Alice Linnane | Associate Producer

Alice works as Senior Producer at the Gate. Alice is passionate about platforming theatre that speaks to different communities in London. She strives to produce work that is inclusive, accessible and that examines the cross sections between the personal, political, global and local. Previously she was Producer at Cardboard Citizens and has produced work with organisations like the National Theatre, Graeae Theatre Company, The Coronet, Barrowland Ballet and more.

Producer credits include: *Bootycandy*, *Hot In Here*, *Brassic FM*, *Wish You Were Here*, *Scenes from the Climate Era* (Gate); *Ruff Tuff Cream Puff Estate Agency* (Cardboard Citizens); *As You Like It* (National Theatre – Public Acts).

Harry Fearnley-Brown for New Wolf Productions | Production Manager

New Wolf Productions are theatrical architects that specialise in harnessing the power of an idea and transforming it into a spectacular and immersive experience. As visual storytellers, New Wolf thrive on pushing the boundaries of traditional theatre production. Serving the theatre and immersive experience markets, New Wolf masterfully connects the dots of a vision to create powerful and compelling stories.

Theatre includes: *Diary of a CEO Live* (UK tour); *Allegiance* (Charing Cross); *Tally's Blood* (UK tour); *Operation Mincemeat*, *Preludes*, *Walworth Farce* (Southwark Playhouse); *Romeo and Juliet* (Shakespeare North Playhouse); *Captain Sandy Live*, *There's No Place Like Home* (Lyric); *Disruption* (Park); *Education Rita* (Perth Theatre and Concert Hall); *Snow Queen* (Trinity).

Roni Neale | Stage Manager

Roni is a stage manager and theatremaker from Dorset, working nationally.

Theatre includes: As Stage Manager: *Consumed* (Lyric Belfast/Park); *Romeo and Juliet* (Theatre Royal Stratford East); *After The Act* (Royal Court); *My Mother's Funeral: The Show* (Edinburgh Fringe Festival/UK tour/NYC/The Yard); *Shanghai Dolls* (Kiln); *English* (RSC/Kiln); *Cowbois* (RSC/Royal Court); *Manic Street Creature* (Southwark Playhouse); *Housemates Festival* (Brixton House); *Hungry* (Soho/Edinburgh Fringe Festival); *Charlie and the Chocolate Factory, Hedwig & the Angry Inch* (Leeds Playhouse).

Writing credits include: *Cinderella* (Rose); *Laika* (rehearsed reading, Camden People's).

Bush Theatre

We make theatre for London. Now.

For over 50 years the Bush Theatre has been a world-famous home for new plays and an internationally renowned champion of playwrights.

Combining ambitious artistic programming with meaningful community engagement work and industry leading talent development schemes, the Bush Theatre champions and supports unheard voices to develop the artists and audiences of the future.

Since opening in 1972 the Bush has produced more than 500 ground-breaking premieres of new plays, developing an enviable reputation for its acclaimed productions nationally and internationally.

They have nurtured the careers of writers including James Graham, Lucy Kirkwood, Temi Wilkey, Jonathan Harvey and Jack Thorne. Recent successes include Tyrell Williams' *Red Pitch*, Benedict Lombe's *Shifters*, and Arinzé Kene's *Misty*. The Bush has won over 100 awards including the Olivier Award for Outstanding Achievement in Affliate Theatre for the past four years for Richard Gadd's *Baby Reindeer*, Igor Memic's *Old Bridge*, Waleed Akhtar's *The P Word* and Matilda Feyiṣayọ Ibini's *Sleepova*.

Located in the renovated old library on Uxbridge Road in the heart of Shepherd's Bush, the Bush Theatre continues to create a space where all communities can be part of its future and call the theatre home.

'The place to go for ground-breaking work as diverse as its audiences' EVENING STANDARD

bushtheatre.co.uk
@bushtheatre

<table>
<tr><td>Artistic Director & Co-CEO</td><td>Taio Lawson</td></tr>
<tr><td>Executive Director & Co-CEO</td><td>Angela Wachner</td></tr>
<tr><td>Outgoing Artistic Director</td><td>Lynette Linton</td></tr>
<tr><td>Outgoing Executive Director</td><td>Mimi Findlay</td></tr>
<tr><td>Executive & Operations Assistant</td><td>Deborah Bahi</td></tr>
<tr><td>Hires & Events Producer</td><td>Zhaleh Bahraini</td></tr>
<tr><td>Technician</td><td>Yuval Brigg</td></tr>
<tr><td>Development Manager</td><td>Choi</td></tr>
<tr><td>Head of Development (maternity leave)</td><td>Jocelyn Cox</td></tr>
<tr><td>People & Culture Manager</td><td>Dorothy Ekema-Walla</td></tr>
<tr><td>Finance Assistant</td><td>Lauren Francis</td></tr>
<tr><td>Head of Technical & Buildings</td><td>Jamie Haigh</td></tr>
<tr><td>Senior Producer</td><td>Emma Halstead</td></tr>
<tr><td>Assistant Venue Manager</td><td>Rae Harm</td></tr>
<tr><td>Head of Finance</td><td>Neil Harris</td></tr>
<tr><td>Marketing & Audience Development Officer</td><td>Karishma Kaur</td></tr>
<tr><td>Box Office Supervisor</td><td>Paula Kramer</td></tr>
<tr><td>Associate Dramaturge</td><td>Frey Kwa Hawking</td></tr>
<tr><td>Community Programme Coordinator</td><td>Joanne Leung</td></tr>
<tr><td>Literary Manager & Lead Dramaturge</td><td>Olivia Poglio-Nwabali</td></tr>
<tr><td>Venue Manager (Theatre)</td><td>Ade Seriki</td></tr>
<tr><td>Press Manager</td><td>Martin Shippen</td></tr>
<tr><td>Head of Community</td><td>Holly Smith</td></tr>
<tr><td>Development Lead</td><td>Ines Tercio</td></tr>
<tr><td>Head of Marketing</td><td>Ed Theakston</td></tr>
<tr><td>Marketing & Digital Officer</td><td>Kelly Thurston</td></tr>
<tr><td>Development Officer</td><td>Amelia White</td></tr>
<tr><td>General Manager</td><td>Camille Wilhelm</td></tr>
<tr><td>Café Bar Manager</td><td>Wayne Wilson</td></tr>
</table>

DUTY MANAGERS
Daniel Cameron, Sara Dawood, George Kirby-Smith, Jacob Meier & Eleanor Wilson.

VENUE SUPERVISORS
Antony Baker, Adryne Caulder-James, Bo Leandro, Nzuzi Malemba, Tatjana Nardone & Asa Wooldridge.

VENUE ASSISTANTS
Emma Chatel, Pyerre Clarke, Georgia Fellows, Daniel Fesoom, Matias Hailu, Taeyun Kim, Ishani McGuire, Ed Mendoza, Dumo Mkweli, Carys Murray, Louis Nicholson, James Robertson, Manuel Ruiz, Ali Shah, Eleanor Stock, Josie Watson, Nefertari Williams, Yemi Yohannes & Joy Zaragoza.

BOARD OF TRUSTEES
Uzma Hasan (Chair), Cllr Stala Antionades, Kim Evans, Daisy Heath, Keerthi Kollimada, Taio Lawson, Anthony Marraccino, Jim Marshall, Rajiv Nathwani, Kwame Owusu, Stephen Pidcock, Catherine Score & Angela Wachner.

Bush Theatre, 7 Uxbridge Road, London W12 8LJ
Box Office: 020 8743 5050 | Administration: 020 8743 3584
Email: info@bushtheatre.co.uk | bushtheatre.co.uk

Alternative Theatre Company Ltd
The Bush Theatre is a Registered Charity
and a company limited by guarantee.
Registered in England no. 1221968 Charity no. 270080

THANK YOU

Our supporters make our work possible. Together, we're evolving the canon and creating a bolder, more diverse, and representative future for British theatre. We're so grateful to you all.

MAJOR DONORS

Charles Holloway OBE
Jim & Michelle Gibson
Georgia Oetker
Rajeev Philip
Cathy & Tim Score
Susie Simkins
Jack Thorne
Gianni & Michael Alen-Buckley

SHOOTING STARS

Jim & Michelle Gibson
Anthony Marraccino & Mariela Manso
Cathy & Tim Score
Susie Simkins

LONE STARS

Clyde Cooper
Adam Kenwright
Jim Marshall

HANDFUL OF STARS

Cyrus Benson
Charlie Bigham
Judy Bollinger
Richard & Sarah Clarke
Christopher delaMare
Sue Fletcher
Thea Guest
Kate Hamer Ltd.
Elizabeth Jack
Simon & Katherine Johnson
Garry & Lorna Lawrence
Phyllida Lloyd & Kate Pakenham
Vivienne Lukey
Sam & Jim Murgatroyd
Georgia Oetker
Mark & Anne Paterson
Miguel & Valeri Ramos Handal
Bhagat Sharma
Dame Emma Thompson
Joe Tinston & Amelia Knott

RISING STARS

Elizabeth Beebe
Martin Blackburn
David Brooks
Catharine Browne
Anthony Chantry
Lauren Clancy
Caroline Clasen
Susan Cuff
Matthew Cushen
Anne-Hélène and Rafaël Biosse Duplan
Austin Erwin
Kim Evans
Mimi Findlay
Jack Gordon
Hugh & Sarah Grootenhuis
Uzma Hasan
Lesley Hill & Russ Shaw
Davina & Malcolm Judelson
Joanna Kennedy
Mike Lewis
Lynette Linton
Tim & Deborah Maunder
Michael McCoy
Judy Mellor
Caro Millington
Rajiv Nathwani
Stephen Pidcock
James St. Ville KC
Jan Topham
Kit & Anthony van Tulleken
Katja van Koten
Angela Wachner

CORPORATE SPONSORS

Biznography
Casting Pictures Ltd.
Nick Hern Books
S&P Global
The Agency

TRUSTS & FOUNDATIONS

Backstage Trust
Buffini Chao Foundation
Christina Smith Foundation
Daisy Trust
Esmée Fairbairn Foundation
Garfield Welson Foundation
Garrick Charitable Trust
The Golsoncott Foundation
Hammersmith United Charities
The Headley Trust
Idlewild Trust
Jerwood Foundation
John Lyon's Charity
John Thaw Foundation
Martin Bowley Charitable Trust
Noël Coward Foundation
Royal Victorial Hall Foundation
The Thistle Trust

And all the donors who wish to remain anonymous.

I'M NOT BEING FUNNY

Piers Black

Acknowledgements

This script is the work of a number of people. The original characters, concept and additional material were created with Jerome Yates and Lucy Karczewski. Prior to rehearsal the script went through dramaturgical development with Bryony Shanahan, Rebecca Prentice and Tia Bannon. Throughout rehearsals the cast and creative team have continued to shape and develop the play towards the production.

Characters

PETER
BILLIE

Notes

– on the end of a line of dialogue indicates an interruption

- occupying a paragraph indicates a beat held by that character

/ indicates a change in direction

. on the end of dialogue indicates commitment to the line

All scenes aligned to the right are flashbacks.

The stand-up scenes should feel like they are taking place in a comedy club.

The exercises should feel alive and dynamic.

The flashbacks should feel cold and real.

Everything else is in their living room.

This text went to press before the end of rehearsals and so may differ slightly from the play as performed.

A microphone in a spotlight.

PETER *enters, seeing audience.*

He goes to the mic.

PETER. Hi. Er –

He taps the mic.

Is this on...?

-

One two, one two?

Is it – Right

-

Hi. Everyone.

This is my first. Yeah –

Should I start? Is it –

-

Okay.

I just? Go. Okay.

-

Right. Erm.

-

My name's Peter. And

-

So I've been working on a joke about spiders recently.

I really think it's got legs.

-

-

Bangs the mic.

Is this – check check?

-

Can I get a bit more juice in my – yeah

-

-

'I really think it's got legs'

(*Fucking hell*)

Tough crowd

-

I did a gig for a bunch of well-done steaks the other day…

Tough crowd

-

Right.

I might. I might actually –

Sorry, I know you've all bought tickets and everything, but I'm not, you know. Don't want to waste anyone's time, so…

-

-

Okay I'm just going to try, here we go. Here we go. Right! Who's ready, who's ready to laugh? Who's ready to laugh and laugh until, until they're sick? Sick up and down the aisles! Who's ready to laugh so much they get stitches – they need stitches, from all the laughing? Laughing so much you rip your mouths wide open, so much that you need stitches on your face from where you've ripped your faces open? Wow, who's ready for THAT? That sounds like fun doesn't it? You'll laugh so much that you'll use up all of your laughter, and then after tonight you'll just be grey, an empty grey mess, bringing greyness everywhere you go, face full of stitches, moving through life unable to find joy, until the people who love you leave because all you do is bring greyness into their lives, and you'll be alone for a long time. For a long, long time. Just you and the grey. The grey that you deserve. The grey where you belong. Grey forever. With the grey getting greyer, until it's not even greyness, it's just. Nothing.

Yeah.

It's gonna be fun!

-

So I've been working on a joke about an octopus recently…

I really think it's got legs

-

(Tentacles) Yeah, very good, got loads of A-levels have you?

-

-

So has anyone heard the one about the comedian who forgets the punchline?

-

-

-

-

-

-

-

-

-

\-

\-

\-

\-

\-

\-

\-

Bangs the mic.

Is this…

Matt, can you just boost the mids? It's not cutting through.

\-

So I've been working on a joke about walnuts recently…

Can't seem to crack it

\-

Come on.

That's –

I think there's something in that

I do

I really do.

I really think there's something in that.

I'm serious.

That's quite – I reckon there's something in that.

\-

Maybe nut

\-

Ruby.

Is that you?

\-

Rubes?

-

So I've been working on a joke about roofs recently…

But it keeps going over everyone's heads

-

So I've been working on a joke about realistic prosthetic limbs recently…

Really think it's legs

-

So I've been working on a joke about killing myself recently…

I just can't work out how to end it

-

-

-

He screams.

-

-

I er –

-

Knock knock?

BILLIE. Who's there?

PETER. OhmyGod! You scared the shit out of me –

BILLIE. Sorry –

PETER. How long have you been there?

BILLIE. I dunno, a while

PETER. Thought you were back late?

BILLIE. Yeah, I'm knackered. I cancelled, and then I didn't want to interrupt. This.

What is this?

PETER. I'm practicing aren't I

BILLIE. I can see that, but. Is this your tight five?

PETER. Yeah.

BILLIE. Okay.

PETER. What?

Is it not funny?

BILLIE. No no yeah it's –

PETER. Fuck's sake

BILLIE. It is! Maybe not, like, in a *traditional* –

PETER. Great.

BILLIE. Do you think it's funny?

PETER. I mean. It's got edges.

BILLIE. Super edgy

PETER. You need so many jokes for five minutes, and it's tomorrow, and five minutes is a long time! Have you timed five minutes? It's really long, and I –

BILLIE. You don't have to do it.

PETER. Do you not think I should?

BILLIE. No! You should, I'm just saying.

PETER. I want to do it. Are you doing yours?

BILLIE. Yeah, I'm excited.

PETER. Is yours ready?

BILLIE. Mine's more like storytelling. Than jokes. Like, funny stories.

PETER. Stories

BILLIE. Yeah and then when people think they're comfortable, wham, pathos. Or like, trauma. I dunno.

PETER. It's an open mic, not a Netflix special.

BILLIE. I know what I'm doing.

PETER. Have you written yours down?

BILLIE. I'm just gonna kind of jam it. How does this work then?

PETER. Oh right. Well, I thought if I moved the sofa back then there'd be more space. And then I was kind of just imagining that the audience is here.

PETER *gestures out.*

And the stage is here.

I dunno how big the actual stage is.

BILLIE. Right.

PETER. I'm using the baby monitor as one of those flashing things that tells you when you're about to finish.

BILLIE. Don't think we get that.

PETER. Karaoke mic. And then for lighting I sort of point the –

BILLIE. Oh yeah that's clever

PETER. Yeah and then when I'm ready I flick the big light off.

And it sort of, happens.

BILLIE. Magic

PETER. Yeah.

Er

-

You weren't meant to. That wasn't for an audience. For anyone.

BILLIE. Okay.

PETER. I'm fine.

-

It's fine. Everything's fine.

BILLIE. Okay.

-

How's she doing?

PETER. Good. Passed out before we finished the first story. Think I just heard her moving about.

BILLIE. How was today?

PETER. Yeah, found a really big stick, scared the shit out of some birds, ate a whole carrot. She is obsessed with the sink. Keeps washing her hands. What three-year-old wants to wash their hands?

BILLIE. A whole carrot?

PETER *nods.*

And? Still nothing?

PETER *shakes his head.*

PETER. Do you want a go then?

BILLIE. Er –

PETER. You signed us up. Least you could do is show me how it's done.

BILLIE. Alright alright alright alright. Are you gonna announce me? Are they gonna do that?

PETER. Yeah, get in the kitchen

PETER *takes the mic and* BILLIE *heads out*

Aaaaaand next up, we have a special act for you, all the way from Planet Thanet, one of our own, please raise your glasses for the delightful, the delicious, the de-lairiest, BILLIE – you got a stage name?

BILLIE. No, just Billie –

PETER. BILLLIIIIEEEEEEEEEE!

BILLIE *appears at the mic.*

BILLIE. Hiiiii! Hi everyone. I'm Billie! Oh wow –

Pointing at mic.

This makes you feel powerful! God I need this in my life. Imagine what I could do if I had this voice all the time. Next time I can't get served at the bar

EXCUSE ME.

Next time I get a spam call

YOUR FAMILY'S ASHAMED OF YOU.

Next time my kid won't fall asleep

SLEEP NOW NIGHT NIGHT SLEEPY TIME.

She mimes strangling a child.

I'm joking, I'm joking!

I would never answer a spam call.

Those guys are annoying.

You know what else is annoying? Traffic lights. It's like, make your mind up! (No that's rubbish, hang on.)

Being sick. That's annoying.

So the other day I'm throwing up what is just liquid pink into a Tesco bag. And *three* men try and help me.

Now that sounds nice, but two of them are also definitely hitting on me.

The other guy gets me a bottle of water and he's trying to explain to me that I have to flick the water on my face, but I'm like up and down, like vomming and coming up for air, and he's like 'You need – to flick – on your face –' And then he's just like, 'Here, I'll do it,' and he starts flicking bits of water at me from this bottle each time I come up, and I'm just –

BILLIE *mimes throwing up and then getting flicked over and over.*

I mean, I can see why the other two guys are interested. Me getting flicked with my bag of pink. I take it home that evening to show Peter, my husband, see if I can get him all riled up –

PETER. Are you er –

BILLIE. What?

PETER. Gonna talk about me?

BILLIE. You and me.

PETER. Right

BILLIE. It's relatable

PETER. Sure. But are you gonna do like, personal stuff?

BILLIE. People need to connect.

PETER. Do you have to?

-

BILLIE. Sorry, you're being a bit shit.

PETER. Okay.

BILLIE. I'm working it out, okay? So can you not like, shit on my routine

PETER. Yeah yeah, sorry. I thought you knew what you were doing –

BILLIE. I need you to like, be my hype man.

PETER. Course!

BILLIE. Like a yes man!

PETER. Yes!

BILLIE. We need to help each other right.

PETER. Yes! We can do it.

BILLIE. Like, let's not go to bed, let's not leave the living room until we've nailed this?

PETER. Yeah!

BILLIE. Deal?

PETER. Deal

BILLIE. Because I don't think either of us have a tight five right now

PETER. No way. I've got like a *loose two*. Maybe not even that.

BILLIE. Go on then, hype me up.

PETER. Right. Woooo! Let's go.

BILLIE. Thank you

PETER. Let's DO IT!

BILLIE. We're doing it! Shall we like, run on the spot or something?

PETER. Yes!

They both run.

Let's warm up our laugh.

PETER *and* BILLIE *face each other and laugh.*

BILLIE. Okay, now look at me. And laugh without smiling.

They try and do this, until:

Hi muffin, Mummy and Daddy are just being insane, don't worry.

PETER. Ruby, it's bedtime. Isn't it?

BILLIE. Do you want a drink? Are you hungry?

PETER. No she's. She's fine.

Because I'm the one who's hungry! I'm going to eat your toes, look out here I –

PETER *lunges forward but is stopped.*

-

-

BILLIE. I'll go.

PETER. Night, Rubes.

BILLIE *leaves* PETER *on his own.*

He inhales, goes to the baby monitor.

We hear BILLIE *putting Ruby to bed.*

She comes back into to the living room.

-

It's okay.

-

PETER. I really need this to work.

I never imagined that the woman breaking my heart would be three years old.

BILLIE. It will.

Hey. You make me laugh. I think you're funny. And she's half me. So…

PETER. So?

BILLIE. So – So! What are the things you do that make me laugh?

PETER. You tell me

BILLIE. Okay, erm, okay okay…

PETER. Fuck me, one at a time –

BILLIE. I'm thinking! Err. There was, there was that one time when –

PETER. 'One time'!

BILLIE. Loads of times! There are loads of times –

PETER. I'm still waiting –

BILLIE. Right, new exercise. Thirty seconds. As many of our funny and embarrassing stories as we can come up with. Ready five, four, three –

PETER. Whoa, wait, just any story, that's –

BILLIE. When we first met, or the first time we went camping, or the first time we –

PETER. First times?

BILLIE. Yeah, go!

They both start writing.

And you can't stop writing.

After a few moments, BILLIE *laughs under her breath. A good memory.*

The following can be felt out / adapted by the actors.

Whilst writing:

PETER. What?

BILLIE. Oh nothing…

PETER. Is it embarrassing? Is it embarrassing about me?

BILLIE. Juuuuust – you concentrate on your own list, mate.

He jumps on an idea and starts writing with pace.

Both writing:

Oh, that is juicy.

BILLIE. What have you got?

PETER. Don't you worry about it, mate. Mate mate mate.

BILLIE. What is it?!

She tries to kick his pen while still writing her own list.

PETER. MATE.

He jumps over the sofa and keeps writing.

A few more moments and then:

BILLIE. Right, times up.

You know what. I think this is it. I think *this* is the tight five.

PETER. Yeah, I dunno.

BILLIE. What?

PETER. I just – ah. I'm not gonna stand up in front of a bunch of strangers and tell stories about you and me.

BILLIE. Why not?

PETER. It's personal. It's weird.

BILLY. What? Are you gonna keep doing shit puns about walnuts?

PETER. You were listening! –

BILLIE. Let's try. First on the list, we're going to have the same thing. Come on, hype man. Commit to the bit. That's what they say.

PETER. 'Commit to the bit'?

BILLIE. Commit to the bit, wooooo!

PETER. Billie. It's not really

BILLIE. It's just. Practise. Nothing's gonna go wrong. Look.

BILLIE *stands and takes the mic.*

BILLIE. 'Lovely being here tonight in, *My Living Room*, thanks for having me. I saw The Kitchen earlier, lovely part of the world. Beautiful crowd, beautiful crowd, my name's – Oh! What was that, sorry? You'd like to hear about how I met my husband?'

PETER. No way –

BILLIE. 'Oh absolutely. You know what. *Funny story*' –

PETER. Seriously?

BILLIE. So. I'm twelve years old. It's the first day back from the summer holidays. And I clock him straight away. Massive head. Like he's filled up from the top down.

PETER. Yeah, straight in with the head jokes.

BILLIE. The Geordie newly arrived in the south. No mates. He's trying to get through the day without drawing attention to himself. But obviously, with his funny accent and massive head, it's hard to keep his head down.

PETER. First off, starting a new school *is* terrifying. Second, my head is actually now –

BILLIE. Try it.

She hands him the mic.

PETER. -

BILLIE. Please?

PETER. -

PETER *stands and takes mic*

-

Big light?

-

'You want to hear about how I met my wife? Alright. Strap in.'

I'm twelve years old. It's my first day at new school. And I clock her straight away.

BILLIE. His shoes aren't right. I don't know what they're doing up there, but it's not the same as down here.

PETER. What the hell?

BILLIE. We're riffing, we're riffing.

PETER. Are you gonna let me –

BILLIE. Yeah, go on.

PETER. Right.

So, it's day one, and I'm trying to understand the new rules. There are three concrete courts where you hang out at lunch. The cool kids hang out at 'Top Court'.

BILLIE. That's me – sorry –

PETER. The boys in the cage and the girls outside it. The losers down on 'Bottom Court'. And everyone else in the middle.

BILLIE. These shoes are the ugliest things you have ever seen. They are not quite shoes and not quite trainers.

PETER. The boys on Top Court are playing football and if the ball gets kicked out then everyone attacks the last person to touch it until they can get it back. There is a big lad called Max who already has chest hair.

BILLIE. Max Pinkerton.

PETER. He picks up the ball and smashes it at a boy with too much hair gel so that it bounces off him and over the cage walls.

BILLIE. BEAAA–

PETER. 'Beats!' Hair Gel runs for his life. He doesn't know that the ball has pelted right into the –

BILLIE. AAAATS. Tuna salad –

PETER. – of a girl on the other side.

She is covered

BILLIE. Coated

PETER. Showered

BILLIE. Swimming

PETER. In tuna salad

BILLIE. Hair. Ears. The lot

PETER. The chase has stopped, everyone's staring and laughing.

Without flinching, she stomps forward in these shoes I've never seen before, and uppercuts Max in front of everyone. Bam. He falls and she turns, marching towards the science block toilets.

BILLIE. School is a war zone. You cannot be a victim.

PETER. And I've never seen power like this. I've never seen such raw…

BILLIE. What?

PETER. Decision making

BILLIE. Oh.

PETER. I'm confused and aroused and scared and I'm following her and I don't know why.

BILLIE. He's following me and I don't know why.

I get to the toilet door and I turn around and he stops and looks at me like a big-headed puppy

PETER. I look at her and –

BILLIE. 'What?'

PETER. She is immortal. Braces. Hair that was once dyed but now looks like rust. Covered in tuna. Her pulse is beating in her neck.

BILLIE. His pulse is beating in the veins in his massive fucking head. Standing there in these butters shoes.

PETER. Drowning in sweat and hormones.

BILLIE. 'Are you following me?'

PETER. 'No! I mean. No.'

BILLIE. 'What are you doing?'

PETER. 'I just – I'm looking for…'

BILLIE. 'What!'

\-

PETER. 'Photocopier'

\-

BILLIE. He says

PETER. 'Photocopier'

BILLIE. And for some reason. That word. In that accent. In that mouth –

PETER. Yeah yeah –

BILLIE. Is the most beautiful thing I've ever heard.

PETER. Oh.

\-

BILLIE. Obviously I don't let him know.

'Why?'

PETER. 'I need to. I'm. I'm printing some flyers.'

BILLIE. 'What flyers?'

PETER. '"Missing" flyers. To help me find it.'

BILLIE. 'Find what?'

And the corner of his mouth twitches.

PETER. 'My tuna salad. Have you seen it?'

BILLIE. But it's not mean. It's like he's releasing a valve in my shoulders and my muscles relax.

And the corner of my mouth starts to lift, and out of nowhere, we're laughing.

PETER. We're laughing together. Not big. Not hooting. Just together.

BILLIE. Well that's not funny.

PETER. No. Should we at least write it down?

BILLIE. No. Five minutes of that? Why is it so hot? I'm sweating. Have we got wine?

PETER. Wine?

Are you sure you –

PETER. Did you give her ice-cream?

-

Did you –

BILLIE. No.

PETER. Why didn't you say no then?

BILLIE. I did.

PETER. You paused

BILLIE. I didn't pause

PETER. You did, I asked you and you didn't say anything

BILLIE. I was thinking

PETER. About what?

BILLIE. Ice cream

PETER. What about it?

BILLIE. I couldn't remember

PETER. If you'd had ice cream?

BILLIE. No –

PETER. No?

BILLIE. We did have ice cream –

PETER. For Christ's – I asked you not to –

BILLIE. But not today

PETER. What? When?

BILLIE. Last week maybe? It was mint chocolate chip

PETER. Mint chocolate chip?

BILLIE. Yeah

PETER. You can remember the flavour but you can't remember the – whatever

BILLIE. What?

PETER. I can't –

BILLIE. What?

PETER. It doesn't matter

BILLIE. It's just ice cream

PETER. But it's not! Is it? It's rules. And boundaries and it's –

BILLIE. Ice cream rules?

PETER. I want to give her ice cream!

BILLIE. Well do it then!

PETER. But I can't just do that whenever I feel like it. We can't – It's *easy*, being the one who gives her treats. You taking her out for a special ice cream taking her to the park, that's the reward for when she does all the boring, shit stuff that I'm making her do. The stuff she doesn't want to do.

-

-

-

BILLIE. I – okay.

PETER. What?

BILLIE. I just want to give her some… I just want her to be happy.

PETER. I know, but –

BILLIE. I know, I know, I'm not – yeah. I'm sorry.

PETER. Okay. Whatever, can we just. Can we go home?
Everyone's looking at us and I fucking hate Pret.

BILLIE. It's fine.

PETER. Right.

-

Okay! Red or white?

BILLIE. Any

PETER. Great. I'm going to have tea. I think.

BILLIE. Knock yourself out.

PETER. Right.

PETER *leaves*.

BILLIE *goes to the microphone*.

BILLIE. Hello! God, that's addictive.

So, this total shitstack has written a book about how many
weeks we all have to live. Not like, this is when the earth is
gonna end, but like this is literally how many weeks you get
in a lifetime.

They reckon the average person gets four thousand weeks.
Of life. Of being alive. And I get what they're doing, making
you visualise a solid thing, like calendar thing, in units, but
come on. Seriously? Who, and at what point in their life,
needs that kind of pressure?

Does the shitstack think that anyone is going to read this
book and feel good about themselves? 'Yeah fantastic look at
all those weeks I've got left to achieve my dreams and enjoy
life to the fullest. Great news, maybe this week I'll go to
bed early and watch *Friends* because I'm actually a little bit

ahead of schedule with my completely achievable life plans you total, total shitstack.'

I'm sure the book is about something else, but I don't have time to read it, do I?

Nothing. *Nothing.* Makes you understand time, like having kids. Losing people and making people. That's when we really get to play laser tag with our old mate mortality.

For a long time I was inconsolable about the fact that I would not get to see Ruby's whole life. Like every parent. And obviously that is the preferred option. But it doesn't make it easier.

PETER *enters.*

PETER. Right, let's go, they're brewing and breathing. What next?

BILLIE. -

PETER. Bills?

BILLIE. Yeah all good.

PETER. Did I interrupt?

BILLIE. No.

No. I'm just thinking.

PETER. Okay. Well, I've also been thinking, getting my creative gooses flying

BILLIE. What?

PETER. I reckon I can get a whole routine out of Ruby's poos. Now I know, when I say it out loud, that sounds –

BILLIE. Childish –

PETER. It's not sophisticated, but I actually think the power dynamic in that situation is quite –

BILLIE. I don't want to do that.

PETER. Well, it doesn't have to be poo, but I think dad jokes could be my thing

BILLIE. Sorry. Can we not.

PETER. Really?

BILLIE. Yeah.

PETER. But –

BILLIE. I just don't want to. I'll do anything, like anything, I'll get up there and do an hour long set on the piles summer of 2023. But I don't want to talk about Ruby.

PETER. I thought this was about her.

BILLIE. For her. She's not the joke. Sorry, is it weird?

PETER. No! It's fine.

-

I would watch that piles set. Just in case you were, you know – Do you want to bounce some material off each other, very gently –

BILLIE. Shut up. 'Creative goose'. You're such a dad.

PETER. WOULD YOU CHANGE IT THOUGH?

They kiss for a moment then BILLIE *breaks off.*

BILLIE. Oh my God, first kiss!

PETER. Hate to break it to you but we've actually done *quite a lot* of kissing –

BILLIE. It's on my list. Let's try it.

PETER. Again –

BILLIE. Let's tag-team it and if it feels like someone's dying then we'll beep in.

PETER. Beep keep it rolling

BILLIE. Beep keep the ball in the air

PETER. Beep we're a team

BILLIE. Beep 'Yes and', that's what they say in improv. 'Yes and' to the situation.

PETER. Beep no idea what that means.

BILLIE. Beep it doesn't matter I'll start.

To the mics.

BILLIE. Right! Sarah Bannister! It's her thirteenth birthday, we're at Thanet Wanderers Rugby Club, and her French mum has put on this incredible spread that no one is eating. Because everyone is thinking about one thing and one thing only.

PETER *and* BILLIE. The Dance.

BILLIE. It is known that a DJ has been booked and that later in the evening he will play a slow song. Almost definitely, but not guaranteed to be, the song from *Titanic.*

It is also known, that when the slow song is played, you HAVE to dance with your girlfriend or boyfriend. Which means at least three and a half minutes of physical contact with the opposite gender.

Someone's older sister told us that the boys might drop their hands down south and touch our bums.

PETER. No way!

BILLIE. Did you beep?

PETER. Beep sorry, but genuinely, someone's older brother told us that we had to drop our hands down south and touch your bums.

BILLIE. We're thrilled

PETER. We're terrified.

BILLIE. Across the county, girls are teaching themselves to stand unnaturally, willing a bubble butt to emerge.

PETER. Beep can I –

BILLIE. Yeah keep the ball up keep it up –

PETER. Me and Billie have been dating.

BILLIE. Errr, beep seeing each other

PETER. We don't use labels

BILLIE. Labels are lame

PETER. Labels tie us down

BILLIE. We have too much other stuff going on for labels

PETER. I wouldn't mind if we gave it a label

BILLIE. I'm so busy with my friends and my hobbies –

PETER. It could be nice

BILLIE. My diary is rammed.

PETER. We wouldn't even have to tell people.

So even though we don't have labels, we are obviously going to slow dance together. Because we are –

BILLIE. But not officially –

PETER. Together.

The fantasy has involved dry ice, laser machines, billowing wind, and every high school prom that we've seen in movies. The reality is Steve. A sweaty man in a Legoland T-shirt who is at least forty.

BILLIE. At least fifty.

PETER. He's too old. Sweaty Steve plays a solid three-hour set with no response.

When, suddenly, the lighting changes. The music stops. There is a collective gut-drop. And the haunting tones of an Irish tin whistle fill the room –

BILLIE. OhmyGodIcanstillfeelit –

PETER. Celine Dion has entered the building.

Steve leers over the PA system. 'Boys and girls. Find your partners.'

It's time.

Billie marches towards me with a slight lilt

BILLIE. I've practised the walk

PETER. She looks at me like she's both sleepy and annoyed

BILLIE. I've practised the look

PETER. And we meet in the middle

BILLIE. I put my hands on his shoulders, he's ninety seven per cent liquid. I'm suddenly aware of my feet. Have I got massive feet? Is this normal? Will Peter notice my feet? What if he trips over them and everyone thinks I tripped him with my massive stupid clown feet and then everyone calls me Flippers for the rest of my life.

PETER. I thank God for the nine-to-fourteen bits of gum I have in my mouth. Guaranteed freshness. But maybe that wasn't enough? Why would I not do at least twenty? I've already fucked it. FUCK. I will never touch a butt.

BILLIE. I will never have my butt touched.

PETER. But then I look up and I see her rusty fringe.

BILLIE. I look up and see his massive head. And we come a little closer. And his sticky body feels nice

PETER. And she smells incredible.

And we feel – right?

BILLIE. Yeah

PETER. Different.

When suddenly. Steve's voice dribbles out of the speakers.

Three words that change our lives forever

BILLIE. 'And now, kiss.'

PETER. This wasn't part of the plan

BILLIE. This wasn't the deal. We're not ready

PETER. Without giving ourselves the time to think, smash our mouths together.

BILLIE. It's wet

PETER. It's sweet

BILLIE. It's hell

-

PETER. Really?

BILLIE. We've come a long way babe

PETER. It's not just the food that's French

BILLIE. Tongues and teeth crash together

PETER. And just as quickly as it started, the chaos ends

BILLIE. NEW RULE. It's got to have grit.

PETER. Grit?

BILLIE. It's got to be funny and it's got to have grit.

PETER. Would have been gritty if you still had braces.

BILLIE. Can you take this seriously? We're wasting time messing around.

PETER. Yeah that's. Okay? Isn't it?

BILLIE. I want it. To feel important.

PETER. I'm trying.

BILLIE. Yeah, I know –

PETER. I am glad we're doing it, I'm excited we're doing it, but I am also like very, very terrified. Which is okay. I think that's normal.

BILLIE. I just want to push it a bit further –

PETER. I think people just want to have a good time.

BILLIE. Yeah, and a provocative time and a challenging time.

PETER. Oh my God, the tea –

PETER *exits*.

BILLIE *has a think*.

She goes to the mic.

BILLIE. Anyone seen *Titanic*? Classic nineties movie.

-

Love that movie. Always wanted to be a French girl.

Always wanted to be more nineties. I was born in the nineties but didn't really get to *live it*. You know what I mean?

-

So I was driving to work the other day and there was this guy on the radio, and I was like, what is this? The nineties?

-

This guy. On the radio.

-

Psssh. Who listens to the radio.

-

Seriously, hands in the air. Who listens to the radio?

-

Okay a few of you. When were these guys born? The nineties?

-

Because you're so in love with your radios.

-

You like this stuff you wait until I get to my bit about CDs.

Hey, you, in the choker and faded jeans, could you beeeee any more nineties?

-

Zing.

Classic nineties joke.

-

Okay, quick poll: when was the best decade for music?

The nineties.

When was the best decade for fashion?

The nineties.

When did the internet come out?

The nineties.

When was Leo DiCaprio in peak condition?

The nineties.

What is a good age to reach?

Nineties!

-

Nineties sounds good.

A solid. Good. Age.

Long enough to see some stuff, get the grand kids through, bit of retirement. Lovely.

-

Twenties. Not so good. Turns out.

As a point to stop.

Actually, quite like hell. Really.

I'm not saying it's the worst. Can't claim that. But it's definitely.

Not.

Good.

-

-

And there's no, like, guide. Of what to do.

So

Sometimes I run…

She speaks a few lines from the chorus of 'Sometimes' by Britney Spears, singing the final line:

(*Singing.*) Baby…

Classic nineties Britney!

PETER. Oh cool, are you doing a musical thing, what's it called, cabaret?

PETER *trips and spills the wine.*

His tea is in a sippy cup.

FUCK

BILLIE. Shhhhhit –

PETER. Fuck fuckfuckfuck

BILLIE. It's alright –

PETER. I was so careful! I had a word with myself before I came in.

BILLIE. It's a superpower. Maybe that should be your routine!

PETER. What, clumsy?

BILLIE. No, slapstick. Mime. Charlie Chaplin sort of thing.

PETER. Maybe

BILLIE. You're good at it. Ruby goes mad for it.

PETER. Hm

BILLIE. You know what I mean. Have you tried that?

PETER. Yeah, it's not – I've tried everything.

BILLIE. Me too.

   Have you tried a double take, she loves a double take –

PETER. Of course I tried a double take. I nearly broke my neck

BILLIE. It's a classic move

   Have you tickled her?

PETER. I think if I tickle her and she doesn't laugh, then my
   heart might fall out

BILLIE. Yeah. Okay. Maybe that's like a last resort.

PETER. That's a code red

BILLIE. Okay.

BILLIE. I don't know how to say this properly. But. I'm sorry?

PETER. Is that a question?

BILLIE. No no I am sorry. Really sorry. And I've been thinking
   a lot. Swimming and thinking. And yeah. I think you were
   probably right. About everything so. Yeah let's do it.

PETER. Do what?

BILLIE. Let's get back together, and –

PETER. Billie I haven't heard from you in –

BILLIE. And have a baby.

-

I don't mean now. Like ten years, twenty years. But yeah.

Are you sure you don't want a cappuccino?

PETER. I –

BILLIE. I'll get you a cappuccino.

PETER. You want to have a baby?

BILLIE. Do they do food here?

PETER. Together?

BILLIE. Yeah.

PETER. Why? Every time we – what's changed?

BILLIE. So I was swimming and thinking and the other day and I got my breath wrong on the flip turn and anyway, I had this thought. When we were together, I really missed myself. Like, a part of myself. I love the part of me that lived with you and had been with you all this time, but there was this other part, like a different me, that could go off into the world and have this different life. And the longer we stayed together, having our life, talking about having kids, the more I missed this other part.

And I think that's why, I didn't want to. Why we're. Not together. Now.

But then when I was in the pool. There was a second where I thought I'd drowned. And I could see it all. See that the part of me that lived with you, the part of me that loves you. I love that part. I REALLY love that part. I would miss that part more than I can imagine missing anything.

I have missed it.

And

Yeah.

If being with you, and having a kid, is what keeps that part of me alive. If that pulls me out of the pool. Then yeah. Let's do it.

> *Long pause.*
>
> PETER. Okay.
>
> BILLIE. Okay?
>
> *Long pause.*

There is this other – It's definitely nothing, but I went to the doctors the other day and –

PETER. That's not classic Britney by the way.

BILLIE. It's her second single?

PETER. It's not exactly 'Toxic'.

BILLIE. Yeah. It's not 'Oops… I Did It Again'. Speaking of, shall we clear that up?

PETER. Yeah, I'll get a –

BILLIE. I actually think the Britney stuff will go down really well with the home crowd.

PETER. Home crowd?

BILLIE. Our mates love Britney.

PETER. Yeah but. Wait. Are you joking? Did you invite –

BILLIE. It'll be fun! They're well excited.

PETER. No way, absolutely not, no way, why would you do that?

BILLIE. Did I not tell you?

PETER. NO!

BILLIE. I did. You should invite people.

PETER. FUCK. How many?

BILLIE. I dunno. Twenty.

PETER. Great. Are the school lot coming?

BILLIE. Course.

PETER. Course they are. And all their partners. Great great great super cool. I'm going to look like a twat in front of everyone and and and we don't have any material!

BILLIE. We've got some. How many pages have you got?

PETER. Well. None. You said not to –

BILLIE. How are we meant to remember –

PETER. I don't know!

Let's. Just. Crack on! Okay?

BILLIE. Are you sure you want to?

PETER. Yes!

BILLIE. It's just. That's probably gonna need some bicarb –

PETER. It doesn't matter. Let's do another one. From the list, come on. First holiday, I'll start.

PETER *takes the mic.*

PETER. It's our first holiday and we go to Portugal. Isn't it lovely. Sun sun sun.

-

Right. You go.

BILLIE. -

Er. Yeah. Our first holiday. We save for ages. My mum's been picking up extra shifts, she gives me eighty euros just before we get on the plane, and we both cry. She tells me to have a good time.

PETER. She tells me to look after you.

-

Sorry. I'd forgotten about that. I'm back.

Shall we – um. Have you got any more exercises for us?

BILLIE. Yeah lets – stream of consciousness. For the time it takes you to finish your tea I'm going to riff on, ahhhh –

PETER. Custard tarts, go!

BILLIE. Oh my God pastel de nata they are little mouthfuls
of heaven I am obsessed with them to the point where I'm
basically comfort eating them because I've accidentally been
learning Spanish instead of Portuguese for the last three
months and the only –

PETER. Time's up. Right, what have you got for me?

BILLIE. How slow do you drink?

The Moorish Castle –

PETER. Yes! I become obsessed with is this Moorish Castle
this incredible building that has been there for hundreds and
maybe thousands of years I'm there with my hands on the
wall thinking about all the hands all those years ago that laid
all these stones that created this that was built to last forever
this thing that's here now the people who built it left a piece
of themselves behind a part of them that will go on through
the centuries and I start thinking will anyone ever use one of
my circuit boards in a hundred years time no way no way in
hell and actually like these days who gets to leave something
behind who gets to put something onto the earth that goes
beyond them –

BILLIE. Beep time's up.

BILLIE *and* PETER *are sat facing forward.*

They wait and wait.

PETER. Are you okay?

BILLIE. Yep.

PETER. You wanna do sudoku?

BILLIE. No

They wait.

PETER. You want something from the machine?

BILLIE *shakes her head.*

You okay?

BILLIE. Still okay. Don't need to keep asking.

PETER. Okay.

-

I might get something from the machine.

They wait.

So nearly went to the wrong hospital

Got the blue book. Was all ready to argue with the midwife.

Saw 'scan' in the calendar and – yeah.

BILLIE. Should introduce my hospitals.

PETER. Yeah

BILLIE. Save them loads of time.

I can do like one big scan for both instead of a – you know.
A happy scan and a scary scan.

PETER. You want me to ask the doctors if –

BILLIE. No

They wait.

PETER. What do you fancy for dinner?

BILLIE. I dunno. Can't think, sorry.

PETER. It's a treat day.

BILLIE. Yeah.

They wait.

Everyone's old.

-

I look like a daughter.
When I go in for bloods everyone's going to think I'm lost.

They wait.

PETER. Sorry.

Wish there was something I could say.

He takes her hand.

They wait.

I'll go to the machine.

PETER. I fucking love that castle.

The baby monitor rattles.

I'll go. Those tiny hands aren't going to wash themselves.

BILLIE. Okay.

PETER *exits.*

BILLIE *goes to the mic.*

BILLIE. It's such a big word.

When you say it.

People are freaked. Fair enough, but –

You end up going through this stage where you have to tell everyone. And it's exhausting. Because it's such a big deal for everyone when they hear it.

To be fair. My husband – He told a lot of people.

But there were loads who I wanted to, you know. I thought it was proper.

There was one woman – I just did a really bad job! I think I was tired, or had like Big Chat fatigue, and I told her at work, and I obviously didn't do 'the speech' properly, so I think I caught her off guard, and she just started sobbing. Like breaking down. Maybe she's got family or something.

Anyway, she's there, bawling her eyes out. And I'm like –

Mimes patting her on the back and giving her a tissue.

And I end up *apologising*. Like, *I'm* consoling *her*.

Supporting her through this difficult time.

'You're going to be okay. Just breathe. Blah blah blah.'

And I start getting a little bit angry. The injustice of it all. And I'm looking at her, thinking…

'You know... There's another big word that begins with C…'

PETER. That's er –

-

Are you sure. You want to do that.

-

BILLIE. Yeah.

PETER. You don't have to.

BILLIE. I don't mind. Doesn't bother me.

PETER. Yeah, but. I'm not saying you shouldn't –

BILLIE. Good.

PETER. I'm just saying. It's a lot.

-

That came out wrong.

I mean. It's a lot for you. In front of a load of people.

BILLIE. So? I'm not gonna be like suddenly reminded.

-

PETER. Okay.

BILLIE. I don't mind being vulnerable.

PETER. What does that mean?

BILLIE. It's easy. Talking about stupid teenage stuff. You should try talking about yourself. Now. Go on, if you're deciding who gets to talk about what.

PETER. Yeah, I don't want to –

BILLIE. Nothing's gonna happen. You won't explode.

PETER. This isn't the place for that.

BILLIE. Where is the place?

PETER. Sorry, I thought we were generating material? The tight five?

BILLIE. Yeah, the tight five –

PETER. So what's this?

BILLIE. It's just – Try, okay? Try it here. Try talking about yourself.

PETER. I can talk about myself

BILLIE. Yeah, 'how's your day' whatever, actually open up.

PETER. I'm fine –

BILLIE. Really? Not feeling a bit, I dunno, 'grey'?

PETER. -

  -

  -

PETER *takes the mic.*

PETER. So.

So I had a job today. Electrician. I'm an electrician. And. And I drove my van to a job, for this, older lady. And. She was really nice. She made me a cup of tea. Two cups. We chatted a bit. I hung around. She. Er.

She didn't want me to leave. I think. She was really nice.

-

BILLIE. And after the job?

PETER. Er. After the job.

I sat in the van.

-

BILLIE. Can you just – Try.

Peter. Just. How I feel?

-

I sat in the van and I felt –

It made me feel –

-

I sat in the van for a really long time.

Because. I –

I didn't –

I wasn't.

-

She was so nice. On her own. And that made me think –

-

I sat in the van for a really long time.

-

Billie, I feel stupid.

Billie?

This isn't helping.

BILLIE. You're doing really well. I thought you were –

PETER. It's not fucking funny is it.

-

BILLIE. Alright?

PETER. It's stupid. No one wants to see that.

BILLIE. Okay, you don't have to –

PETER. Why are you making me then?

BILLIE. Not making you do anything –

PETER. You are, you're making me, like a performing monkey, you're making me, tomorrow I have to stand up in front of a load of people, and like suddenly be hilarious, and that's actually my idea of hell. Actually.

Because it's not funny.

Nothing's funny.

BILLIE. Do you need to go for a walk or –

PETER. No I don't need to go for a walk. It's – there's – look, I feel like I don't know where I am, okay?

BILLIE. Okay

PETER. Sometimes I'm over here, and other times I'm over here, and sometimes I have no idea where you are!

BILLIE. Where I am?

PETER. I just need to be in the middle, and, and it's hard – it's hard – but I know it's harder for you, obviously, so much harder, so I don't want to –

-

I know it's harder for you.

BILLIE. Are you sure you don't want to go for a walk?

PETER. No!

-

Thank you.

-

Sorry.

-

-

-

BILLIE. Right. Well. I'm gonna. I'm gonna go for a walk.
Around the block.

BILLIE *exits.*

Long pause.

He tidies.

He breaks.

He looks at the baby monitor.

He goes to the mic.

PETER. She had these bright red gums when she was born. And
lots of babies don't smile – no one ever told me this – that
for ages babies don't smile or laugh or whatever. They make
noises and stuff but the actual smiling and happiness, that
takes a while. But Ruby was really early, for some reason.
And she would open her mouth with these big gums and just
beam. We called them her ruby reds.

And when she started laughing, it was like crack. This noise
coming out of her. It's just the best best noise I've ever
heard. And I know I'm her dad and everything, but I really
do think, objectively, it's the best sound in the world. It's
like.

It's like

Like brilliant jewels.

Like this magic red light is pouring out of her mouth and
filling the room.

And yeah. So she hasn't smiled. Or laughed. Since we told
her about her mum.

-

She's little. So we simplified it. But she got it.

-

And I guess we. Billie. Was hoping. That this. Doing this.
If we could make a room full of people laugh. That would
make it easier.

Less scary.

Less uh –

But I'm still.

I'm still scared.

-

-

I'm really scared.

BILLIE *enters.*

She goes to PETER *and gives him a little squeeze.*

BILLIE. You okay?

PETER *nods.*

Is she okay?

PETER *nods.*

Look I –

-

BILLIE. Oh my God, now now –

BILLIE *gestures for* PETER *to come over, one hand on her*
stomach.

PETER. Now?!

BILLIE. I can feel something, I can definitely feel something

Put your hand there.

PETER places his hand on BILLIE*'s stomach.*

Can you feel something?

Wait while he feels with eyes closed.

PETER *gasps. Joy.*

He looks up at her, amazed.

PETER. I can feel something

BILLIE. My husband… He's.

He's a little uptight at the moment!

'God if you love control so much you should have married it!'

No, I'm. He's great.

He's not always like this. Used to be this silly, goofy. Clown.

We're having a bit of. We've had a tricky time recently. Our daughter. I'm not talking about that. But before that, he was less bothered about. Controlling things.

Loosey goosey.

There was this one time. Little while ago now.

I come home after a long day at work, and as I'm putting my bags down he suddenly crashes around the corner panting and cackling like an idiot, wearing a colander on his head. And I can hear my daughter screeching in the garden, having the best time, and he literally hasn't done a single fucking thing he was meant to do that day, like he was meant to put on a wash and drop off our neighbour's parcel, and do some actual work, but he hasn't done a single thing, and he's so happy, and I walk in with this shitty mood, and the moment I collide with this grinning, kitchen-wear-ing maniac, I'm just-

I was just

Like

It's all going to be okay.

Really

The important stuff is going to be okay

And everything else doesn't matter.

PETER. I'm sorry, I didn't –

BILLIE. I'm sorry.

PETER. I'm not angry, I'm –

Let's. Come on. We can do this.

BILLIE. Peter –

PETER. I find it hard to find the right words sometimes. But I want to –

BILLIE. It's okay

PETER. I'm happy to talk. About me, and us. But there are some things I don't want to, if that's okay?

BILLIE. Of course.

PETER. Not like this. In front of people. It's fine if you want to, but.

BILLIE. Yeah.

PETER. And we should, talk about it. You and me.

BILLIE. Yeah, I think that's good.

PETER. Not now. We're running out of time to, you know. Let's get this done!

BILLIE. We've got time.

PETER. I don't want to scare you, but unless you're okay with doing Saturday morning soft play on no sleep, we don't have time.

BILLIE. We've got time.

PETER. Really?

BILLIE. Say it.

PETER. So. I feel like I'm – we're on a pendulum.

BILLIE. A pendulum –

PETER. Bear with me. And there are times when things are great and you're feeling good and we are kind of ignoring everything, and we start making plans for the future and thinking that things might be like normal, and then suddenly we'll be watching a movie which has a sick-mum storyline or everything fucking everything that throws illness in like it's some button you press to get a reaction, and it's just a Thursday and we're eating noodles and suddenly, bang, because someone in an air-conditioned room in LA is lazy, we're being made to look at this thing right in the face, the thing we don't want to look at, and because we've done such a good job of ignoring it –

BILLIE. I'm not ignoring it –

PETER. It means that we get. Whiplashed. Into it. And the pendulum swings to the other side where things aren't good. And it's all we think about. And we don't want to eat noodles on a Thursday. Well, I don't. I don't want to do anything. I'm just. Scared. And the fact that there are people out and about going to parties and doing shopping, seems absurd. And I think the only way we can live is when the pendulum is right in the middle. At this very thin point, bang in the middle, where it's not ignoring it completely, and it's not being paralysed by it. We're putting it on a lead and bringing it into the room with us, but we're not letting it sit on the sofa. While we eat noodles. On a Thursday.

It's not a science

BILLIE. Okay. Where are you now?

PETER. I feel like watching you get up in front of everyone we know and make jokes about it. That might swing pretty hard in one direction.

BILLIE. Yeah. Okay.

I appreciate this isn't just happening to me. I mean. The hardest part of this. Is you. And Rubes. Being responsible for that –

PETER. Billie –

BILLIE. But also. It is. Happening to me. And I want to laugh at it. I want to get a big spotlight and go, 'You're a fucking joke, mate.' Because it's not going to be any different. If I laugh or cry, or spend a year travelling the world or a year locked in our bedroom. I know about the pendulum. Of course I do! It's my pendulum! I know it feels good to ignore it, and I know that the longer I ignore it the more it's going to punish me. And I know if I let it take over it's not good, like I don't want to be in that place. But I'm exhausted, Pete. With constantly checking in, to see where I'm at. I feel so removed. From life. Because I am living in this big picture space all the time. Got to be grateful for every second but also can't be sad about how few seconds are left. Got to try and live life to the fullest even though my meds make me exhausted. Love the NHS for giving me the most incredible treatment and doctors for free, but also can't believe how inefficient and painful their systems are – I got put through to a lift yesterday! I was being bounced around to all these different departments and someone connected me to the intercom in a lift –

PETER. Like an elevator?

BILLIE. I was ranting about trying to change this fucking appointment and someone was like, 'Sorry you're in a lift' –

PETER. What the actual –

BILLIE. What I'm saying is that this pendulum swinging, constant balancing act, of zooming in and out, being squeezed and free falling – I know. Mate.

PETER. I know you know –

BILLIE. I'm paying into a pension! How fucked is that?

PETER. Billie –

BILLIE. I'm so.

Tired.

-

-

PETER. So what do you want to do?

BILLIE. I want her to laugh again.

PETER. Me too.

BILLIE. Maybe it's stupid. But I think this will work.

PETER. You know she can't be in the room when we do it.

BILLIE. I just think it will be good for us.

And like if we push. And make it happen. Then it'll be. Like proof.

-

PETER. Then let's do it.

BILLIE. Yeah?

PETER. Yeah.

BILLIE. Fuckmeokay –

PETER. Can I make a request?

BILLIE. Sure

PETER. I know you don't want to talk about Ruby, I get that, but I do think for me, it's like a gold mine –

BILLIE. I really really really don't want to –

PETER. Okay, I hear that, but how about 'parenting', because I'm pretty sure you've got a few things to say about –

BILLIE. Pregnancy! Fucking hell. Has anyone seen *Alien*? You know what's really mad about pregnancy, is that when it comes to an end, instead of recovering, you have to give birth!

PETER. Alright, tag me in, I'm locked and loaded, who's ready for some mature comedy?!

BILLIE. Is this the poo section –

PETER. My baby promised, she swore that she wouldn't ruin my favourite white T-shirt. Looked me in the eye, shook my hand and everything.

But I know she's full of shit.

PETER. I play this game with my daughter where I hide her poos. Steal them out of her nappy in the night. The other day she was so angry, furious, just completely seeing red. I was genuinely scared.

Fair enough. She lost her shit.

Do you wanna tag back in?

BILLIE. No you're on a roll

PETER. I'm sifting I'm sifting finding the gold

BILLIE. Gotta find that nugget

PETER. Okay okay. So the other day, my daughter accidentally pooped in the hallway, and she was all flustered, she was so upset about how we were going to clean it up, because apparently it's going everywhere, spreading out, and she was getting really overwhelmed.

And I was like 'get your shit together'

No I'm joking I'm joking. I wouldn't change a single scream-filled night. I wouldn't change a moment of the poo-catching, vomit-dodging, sticky-handed, hair-pulling, car-sicking, trauma-bonding experience.

No. Seriously.

It's the most mad, and breathtaking thing ever. It's so much all the time. You feel everything, all the time.

Because it's living.

He hears himself.

Well it is!

All the time.

And yeah we made a huge decision, and Billie, even if at first she wasn't – she didn't –

She's the best mum in the world.

I cannot believe the, the depth. Of her well.

And now.

I will always have a little part of her.

-

And Ruby? Pfft. Stop it. Shut up right now.

Look, at the end of the longest day, and she finally goes to sleep, and we finally crash on the sofa, the first thing I do is get my phone out and look at photos of her.

BILLIE. I don't want to talk about her

PETER. Yeah but –

BILLIE. I specifically said that I don't want to talk about her –

PETER. Okay but you also said you want it to be hilarious and gritty and important and not about being a teenager and you stopped me talking about a a a castle so there are quite a lot of rules –

BILLIE. Okay, forgive me for having an opinion, one of us has to.

PETER. Oh, I have opinions, like 'I don't want to do stand-up'. Like, 'I definitely don't want to do stand-up in front of your shit mates.'

BILLIE. Wow.

PETER. I don't know why I said that.

BILLIE. No great, that's good to know.

PETER. It's just Lucy's boyfriend I don't like.

BILLIE. Why don't you sit tomorrow out.

PETER. No, I'm doing it

BILLIE. No it's fine I'll just do it

PETER. You just write down exactly what you want me to say –

BILLIE. I've actually just had a wave of inspiration. Yeah you've inspired me. I've got an idea, for a bit. Are you ready, this is gonna be really good. Really gonna crack some people up. Here, strap in for a proper laughter tsunami –

BILLIE. Four to six years.

Four to six years.

Four to six years is a mad amount of time to make sense of.

Because it's not like now. But it is happening.

Four to six years.

One world cup and half an Olympics.

Four to six years.

Or maybe longer! One doctor said ten at one point. Depending on how the science moves. I like that doctor.

Four to six years.

Enough time to make some pretty big decisions.

FOUR. TO. SIX. YEARS.

Decisions about a whole other human being.

FOUR. TO. SIX. YEARS.

A decision that when you thought about it, you wouldn't say you'd been 'coerced', but maybe 'pushed' or 'nudged'.

FOUR. TO. SIX. YEARS.

A decision that is irreversible.

FOUR. TO. SIX. YEARS.

A decision that you may or may not feel overwhelmingly guilty about for the rest of your medically limited life.

FOUR TO SIX –

      BILLIE. I can definitely feel something

PETER. Are you okay? Do you wanna stop?

      PETER. I think I can feel something

BILLIE. FOUR TO SIX YEARS /

      PETER. Oh yeah, she'll do

      BILLIE. What's that smell? /

PETER. Should we get the most expensive one or do they all work the same?

    BILLIE. It's not a covid test, get the expensive one /

      PETER. And that? That's a heartbeat?

      BILLIE. Oh my God

      PETER. That's a heartbeat! /

      BILLIE. I'm trying mate /

PETER. It looks like a paprika bomb's gone off in there /

BILLIE. FOUR TO SIX YEARS /

PETER. Are you – Are you having another? /

BILLIE. Okay okay okay, I feel like everyone is kinda skirting around-around. Like. What does that actually mean?

PETER. Billie –

BILLIE. No, can someone just say it. How long? /

PETER. Just a lick of paint

BILLIE. What's a lick?

PETER. About this much /

Sorry, 'Four to six years'?

BILLIE. Cool cool cool cool cool cool cool cool cool cool /

PETER. Do we need the car seat attachment?

BILLIE. Yeah probably

PETER. I think definitely

BILLIE. But we're going to get everything on Vinted /

PETER. Put it down, Ruby.

BILLIE. Please. Please. No one's angry. Just put it /

PETER. That's hilarious /

BILLIE. FOUR TO SIX YEARS /

PETER. You're so funny /

BILLIE. Like, let's not go to bed, let's not leave the living room until we've nailed this? /

PETER. Yeah!

BILLIE. Deal?

PETER. Deal /

Where are you gonna go?

BILLIE. I don't know!

PETER. Are you staying here?

BILLIE. I haven't thought about that!

PETER. Well, if you need to –

BILLIE. Stop being – stop doing – I don't need you to do that. /

PETER. So we're getting a second opinion /

BILLIE. FOUR TO SIX YEARS /

PETER. Are you okay?

BILLIE. I told you I don't want to make jokes about Ruby.

PETER. I'm not making jokes about her! I'm trying to help.

BILLIE. Come on then. Let's have another HAPPY memory. Another blissful, nostalgic –

PETER. Look, I'm sorry –

BILLIE. Why don't we talk about the first time we held hands, or the first time we accidentally wore the same outfit, or or –

PETER. Are you okay?

BILLIE. STOP. Asking me if I'm okay. From now on you can just always assume I'm okay unless I specifically tell you that I'm not. Okay? ARE YOU OKAY WITH THAT?

-

-

First flat. Let's go.

BILLIE *picks us the mic.*

She faces PETER.

BILLIE. We've had the chat, we've made the plan. Each of us has outgrown our childhood bedrooms and as much as we love having our washing done for us, it's a faff having to bang quietly. So we're moving in together.

-

-

Come on then.

PETER. I don't.

Are we done. With this –

BILLIE. Peter is much more excited about this than I am.

-

Aren't you?

-

PETER. What are you doing?

BILLIE. We. Are generating material. Hilarious material. Everyone is going to laugh. Haha.

PETER. -

-

-

BILLIE. Peter. My now-husband. Is more excited about it than I am. Aren't you?

PETER. -

He eventually picks up the mic.

They both face in.

I'm excited to create a space of our own.

BILLIE. But mainly we're excited to stop having to bang quietly.

We bite the bullet and eventually find a tiny little place, owned by a private landlady

PETER. Who has no idea how much she could be charging

BILLIE. With big windows and parquet floors

PETER. It's unfurnished so we slowly start filling it with our own bits. Everyone helps

BILLIE. Mum is trying to be upbeat but I know how hard it is for her.

PETER. That's not how I remember it. She was begging me –

BILLIE. No she wasn't –

PETER. Finally get a bit of space –

BILLIE. Don't. Don't do that.

\-

PETER. What?

BILLIE. That isn't what happened is it. So stop –

PETER. I'm joking

BILLIE. Well don't. That's my mum.

PETER. So I can't talk about your mum either –

BILLIE. No you can't –

Peter is thrilled about the whole picture. He wants to tie this down, he wants to get in line for a lifetime membership to joint bank accounts and sensible coats and normal, just normal –

PETER. She says 'boring'.

BILLIE. Queuing up to go down the slide of forgettable mediocrity.

PETER. 'Our life is boring'

BILLIE. And I know that for Peter, moving in together is one step closer to the front of this queue.

PETER. Which for someone who has worked quite hard at building this life

BILLIE. And all steps lead towards the big three.

PETER. Someone who really enjoys it.

BILLIE. Marriage. Kids. Death.

PETER. Who loves it. Actually.

BILLIE. Living in my hometown, and hitting the big three.

PETER. It's quite hard to hear.

BILLIE. To be fair to him, it does make sense.

PETER. It's convenient.

BILLIE. That's romantic.

PETER. It can be convenient and romantic.

BILLIE. No, you're right. It's convenient, financially smart, and sensible, and boring –

PETER. There it is.

BILLIE. I want to travel the world, and go to uni, and –

PETER. But you don't.

-

You don't do that.

BILLIE. Ouch.

PETER. Do you?

-

Go on then?

BILLIE. -

-

PETER. Go on.

BILLIE. What are you –

PETER. Leave.

BILLIE. I'm not leaving.

PETER. Leave us then.

If you'd rather not be here.

BILLIE. -

Are you joking?

PETER. We'll be fine without you.

BILLIE. -

BILLIE. You're right. It's not fucking funny. I'm done.

BILLIE *sits.*

-

-

-

PETER. Hey?

-

I – I obviously didn't mean –

PETER *doesn't know what to do.*

It's okay.

BILLIE *turns away.*

Long pause.

Beep?

Nothing.

PETER *goes to her and gives her a hug, wrapping his legs around her.*

They sit like this for a while.

Oh!

PETER *jumps up and fiddles with his phone. He lowers the lights.*

'My Heart Will Go On' by Celine Dion starts to play.

BILLIE *smiles, despite herself.*

'Boys and girls…'

BILLIE. Yeah yeah yeah

BILLIE *gets up and goes to* PETER.

They slow dance for a while.

Just being together.

PETER. 'And now' –

BILLIE. Noooooo!!! –

PETER. 'Kiss'

They laugh.

They kiss.

The kiss becomes charged. Physical. A way of communicating.

BILLIE *cries.*

She pulls away, real panic.

Hey hey, what's wrong?

BILLIE. Fuck I can't breathe –

PETER. It's okay it's okay –

BILLIE. I'm fine I'm fine, I just –

I want to see it. Everything she does. First kiss, holiday, first flat, first – everything. And I'm going to miss it. I'm going to miss everything.

PETER. We don't know –

BILLIE. But we do. And she's going to grow up without a mum. And that's my fault. We knew what was going to happen, but we did it anyway. That's not fair.

PETER. She'd rather be alive, and have you for a bit, than not be here at all.

BILLIE. She's all messed up already! What three-year-old can't laugh?!

PETER. You've given her everything.

BILLIE. You don't think she's gonna be all messed up?

PETER. Like her mum? Look. You're right. None of this is funny. And we can do gratitude and we can do counselling and we can take it a day at a time. But really. It's just fucked.

BILLIE *nods.*

That's it. It's well and truly, completely fucked.

BILLIE. Yeah.

PETER. And yeah, everything looks bad, and everything is pointing one way. And also. At the same time. We don't know what's going to happen. We don't know what's going to happen tomorrow. You could get hit by a bus, or a scientist could have a mad breakthrough. We don't know.

BILLIE. I just want her to be happy.

PETER. I know.

BILLIE. I want to see everything. And I want her to be happy.

-

BILLIE *nods.*

PETER. Look. Let's do them now.

BILLIE. Do what?

PETER *pulls away and takes a breath.*

PETER. It's Ruby's first day of school.

BILLIE. Pete, I don't think I can –

PETER. We wake her up together.

BILLIE. Pete, please –

PETER. I cook her favourite, choppy egg.

-

You take on teeth cleaning

-

BILLIE *shakes her head.*

I get her bag ready. Tiny pencil case. Ridiculous stationery.

-

You put her outfit together. Dinosaur jumper and red skirt –

BILLIE. I'd never do that. The clash –

PETER. Come on. I need your help.

BILLIE. I just –

PETER. Hype man?

-

-

BILLIE. -

PETER. We take her to the gates, ready for the waterworks, and she swans in like she owns the place.

BILLIE *smiles.*

PETER. You okay?

BILLIE *nods.*

BILLIE. Right.

Ruby lies for the first time. An expert tells us that this is a sign of intelligence.

PETER. No way!

Ruby's first visit from the tooth fairy. Ruby says she's not as pretty as she thought she'd be. You are heartbroken.

BILLIE. You accidentally swear at her first parents evening. I find it very attractive.

PETER. Ruby takes singing lessons. She learns to hum, chant and yodel. She is a sensation.

BILLIE. You're a contestant on *The Chase* and are beaten in an unremarkable final round.

PETER. Tuna fishing is banned globally. You celebrate with a salad.

BILLIE. Ruby finds the drawer in the kitchen above the cupboard that she's not allowed to go into. We have a bad day.

PETER. You are an exact genetic match for a new medical trial that could extend your life by ten years.

\-

\-

BILLIE *nods.*

BILLIE. We go on holiday near Cardiff and it rains solidly for six days. On the seventh day, we are given light, and the most glorious sunshine breaks across the valley. It is bright purple. None of us have seen anything like it.

PETER. We hold a funeral service for the family gerbil –

BILLIE. Grogory.

PETER. Ruby sings 'God Save the King' followed by 'Don't Stop Moving' by S Club 7.

BILLIE. The service takes forty-five mins and has six costume changes.

PETER. Ruby dyes her hair red. It looks like it's always been that colour.

BILLIE. Ruby finds a golden ticket in a chocolate bar and we all go to a factory for a free tour. It is traumatic, many people are injured, but after years of therapy we come out the other side stronger as a family.

PETER. Ruby accidentally says 'I love you' to us in front of all of her mates. She is mortified and we dine out on it for six months.

BILLIE. You rupture your Achilles getting out of the shower. We have the best day in A&E, eating flapjacks and watching the big telly on mute.

PETER. You respond well to the medical trial. It goes through all the necessary phases to become a recognised form of treatment.

BILLIE. Despite some wobbly A-levels, Ruby goes to uni. Dropping her off, we cry the whole car journey home.

PETER. Ruby's wedding day.

BILLIE. Oh God –

PETER. Ruby looks just like her mam. I stroke her thumb as I walk her down the aisle. We love her fiancé, they've got soft eyes and strong hands.

BILLIE. We see a woman in a white dress who is so much more than both of us.

PETER. We see a woman in a white dress who is surrounded by family and friends.

BILLIE. So many friends –

PETER. We all absolutely adore her.

BILLIE. And even though today we are both sort of celebrities, 'Ruby's mum' –

PETER. 'Ruby's dad' –

BILLIE. We can't stop crying.

PETER. Dancing and crying.

BILLIE. You undergo extensive reconstructive surgery after re-rupturing your Achilles.

PETER. Wow my Achilles takes a battering

BILLIE. You are invited back onto *The Chase* and wipe the floor with the expert.

PETER. You get the all clear.

-

-

All clear –

BILLIE. All clear –

PETER. All clear –

BILLIE. ALL CLEAR –

PETER. ALL CLEAR BABY.

BILLIE. ALL FUCKING CLEAR.

PETER. We celebrate our twenty-fifth wedding anniversary. All our friends come for a big meal. The nurses who helped you through your treatment also come.

BILLIE. We become grandparents.

PETER. We are invited by NASA to be the first family to live on Mars.

BILLIE. We break records all the time. Everything we do makes us the first people to do that thing on another planet.

PETER. We become the most famous people 'from Earth'.

BILLIE. But we keep our privacy.

PETER. And we stay humble.

BILLIE. Custard tarts to eat.

PETER. Electrics to install.

BILLIE. We have access to new materials.

PETER. New knowledge.

BILLIE. New ideas.

PETER. We learn to fly.

BILLIE. We learn to breathe the atmosphere.

PETER. We move to Jupiter.

BILLIE. We holiday in Saturn.

PETER. We play

BILLIE. And we soar

PETER. And we laugh –

Ruby's baby monitor glows red and we hear a giggle.

PETER *and* BILLIE *freeze.*

BILLIE. And we laugh?

The monitor glows red again, a full giggle.

PETER. We laugh

BILLIE. And we laugh

A full laugh. Beams of red light.

PETER. And we laugh –

BILLIE. And we laugh –

PETER. And we laugh –

BILLIE. And –

Huge laughter erupts from everywhere.

Red light pours out of every surface.

An intense burst of sound and light.

PETER *and* BILLIE *bathe in it.*

Blackout.

Coda / Call-Back

PETER *and* BILLIE *are on the cliffs over Stone Bay.*

BILLIE *has Ruby strapped to her front as a newborn.*

PETER. Do you want me to –

BILLIE. No, I've got her

How's she doing?

PETER *checks.*

PETER. Great. Beaming.

BILLIE. Are you beaming? Are you *beaming?*

Long, good pause.

BILLIE. You know. We could never go back to work?

Just sayin'

PETER. Okay…

Okay. Reckon if we really tightened. Trimmed and tightened.

Then yeah, we could make it work.

BILLIE. What are you thinking?

PETER. Well the baby, she's gotta go.

BILLIE. No!

PETER. Yeah, first thing.

BILLIE. But we just got her.

PETER. I know but that thing is a cash drain. Gotta ditch her.

BILLIE. Aw man. Well okay, if we have to.

PETER. Sorry about that. And I guess next we'd have to have a serious look at our pudding and treats budget.

BILLIE. Whoa. That, I am less chill about.

PETER. Have you seen the price of Rolo yoghurt these days?

BILLIE. State of this country.

PETER. It's unforgivable.

BILLIE. Wait are you saying *less* treats, or *no* treats?

PETER. Well how long do you wanna be off work babe?

BILLIE. Man. Okay. What next. I've already given up drinking

PETER. Very good.

BILLIE. Though actually, if we don't have the baby anymore, then I'm definitely gonna drink.

PETER. These are the sacrifices you have to make if you want a life of leisure.

BILLIE. Hmm.

Not much point having loads of time if you can't do anything fun with it.

PETER. You can sit. Here. You can watch the sea. With me. That's all free.

BILLIE. Yeah.

Okay. Let's stay off work, for as long as possible, really tight and really trim. But can we have the baby back?

PETER. Yeah alright.

BILLIE. Just you and me. And the baby. And as much time as possible.

A Nick Hern Book

I'm Not Being Funny first published in Great Britain as a paperback original
in 2026 by Nick Hern Books Limited, The Glasshouse, 49a Goldhawk Road,
London W12 8QP, in association with the Bush Theatre, London

I'm Not Being Funny copyright © 2026 Piers Black

Piers Black has asserted his right to be identified as the author of this work

Cover photograph: Richard Lakos

Designed and typeset by Nick Hern Books, London
Printed in Great Britain by Mimeo Ltd, Huntingdon, Cambridgeshire PE29 6XX

A CIP catalogue record for this book is available from the British Library

ISBN 978 1 83904 571 4

CAUTION   All rights whatsoever in this play are strictly reserved. Requests to
reproduce the text in whole or in part should be addressed to the publisher.

Amateur Performing Rights   Applications for performance, including
readings and excerpts, by amateurs in the English language should be addressed
to the Performing Rights Department, Nick Hern Books, The Glasshouse,
49a Goldhawk Road, London W12 8QP, *tel* +44 (0)20 8749 4953,
email rights@nickhernbooks.co.uk, except as follows:

Australia: ORiGiN Theatrical, *email* enquiries@originmusic.com.au,
web www.origintheatrical.com.au

New Zealand: Play Bureau, 20 Rua Street, Mangapapa, Gisborne, 4010,
tel +64 21 258 3998, *email* info@playbureau.com

United States and Canada: Rochelle Stevens & Co, see details below

Professional Performing Rights   Rights Applications for performance by
professionals in any medium and in any language throughout the world
should be addressed in the first instance to Rochelle Stevens & Co,
2 Terretts Place, Upper Street, London, N1 1QZ *tel* +44 (0)20 7 359 3900
email info@rochellestevens.com

No performance of any kind may be given unless a licence has been obtained.
Applications should be made before rehearsals begin. Publication of this play
does not necessarily indicate its availability for amateur performance.

www.nickhernbooks.co.uk/environmental-policy

Nick Hern Books' authorised representative in the EU is
Easy Access System Europe – Mustamäe tee 50, 10621 Tallinn, Estonia
email gpsr.requests@easproject.com

www.nickhernbooks.co.uk

@nickhernbooks